Komm mit!®

TPR Storytelling Book

HOLT, RINEHART AND WINSTON

A Harcourt Classroom Education Company

Austin · New York · Orlando · Atlanta · San Francisco · Boston · Dallas · Toronto · London

Contributing Writers

Diane E. Laumer

Carol Gaab

Cover Photo/Illustration Credits
Mask/ribbons: Scott Van Osdol; students: George Winkler/HRW Photo; illustration: Bob McMahon

Art Credits
All illustrations created by Bob McMahon.

KOMM MIT! is a trademark licensed to Holt, Rinehart and Winston, registered in the United States of America and/or other jurisdictions.

Printed in the United States of America

ISBN 0-03-065479-3

8 9 10 11 018 11 10 09 08

Contents

To the Teacher

TPRS, once referred to as Total Physical Response Storytelling, has evolved into a methodology that is more accurately described as Total Physical Reading and Storytelling. TPRS experts around the globe have collaboratively honed a highly successful methodology which facilitates unrivaled fluency, listening and reading comprehension skills, and writing fluency.

A common-sense approach to learning and teaching language, TPRS facilitates a *natural* order of acquisition. While many methods focus prematurely on activities which require *output* (production in the form of writing or speaking), TPRS focuses on *input* by providing a myriad of "input-based activities" *before* students are required or expected to speak and/or write. Successful TPRS practitioners focus on providing an inordinate amount of Comprehensible Input (CI) through auditory and written means. In other words, the learner is exposed to planned, sequential and repetitive language structures through listening to and reading stories. Students focus on entertaining and engaging stories, rather than on consciously learning or memorizing vocabulary items.

Because TPRS is a multi-sensory methodology, it meets the needs of various learning styles. Gestures and acting, for example, meet the needs of kinesthetic learners; visual images (illustrations, props, puppets, live actors, and so on) satisfy the needs of visual learners; the tremendous amount of contextualized, *comprehensible* input appeals to visual and auditory learners. Students develop a real "ear for the language," learning to listen and respond to what *sounds* right.

TPRS promotes skills and activities that appeal to the right hemisphere of the brain, the hemisphere that dominates during early stages of language acquisition. The right brain processes body language, intonation, speech melody, visual imagery, and so on. These stimuli, which are inherent in TPRS, help the language learner decipher and make meaning of messages, resulting in rapid internalization, acquisition, and fluency. TPRS delays (not eliminates) the introduction of discrete grammar, which is a left-brain function. This is essential to avoid a raised affective filter and a hypersensitive speech monitor, two conditions that impede acquisition and delay fluency.

The following pages provide step-by-step instructions for successfully and easily implementing the steps to TPRS. Although it is important to complete each step, it is not necessary to do each and every activity listed within each step (with the exception of READING!). Numerous suggestions are given to provide variety and avoid monotony in the classroom.

There are three basic steps to TPRS:

1. **Teach new vocabulary structures.**
2. **Use the new structures in a story.**
3. **Revise the story and intensify acquisition.**

Step One:
Teach new vocabulary structures.

Begin by selecting three vocabulary items from the (new) vocabulary list. New vocabulary structures may consist of an individual word or an entire phrase and should be introduced and practiced in a state that is natural to speech. For example, nouns are introduced with the appropriate article, expressions and idiomatic phrases are introduced in their entirety, and verbs are introduced in a conjugated state, one verb form at a time.

Practice should focus on one verb form at a time, regardless of the tense that is being taught. Typically, teachers tend to teach according to the grammar syllabus, rather than according to what is naturally used most frequently in speech. In other words, although it is much more common to communicate in the past tense, the present tense is typically taught first. Whatever the tense, begin formal instruction with one verb form at a time.

Each of the three new vocabulary structures should be introduced one at a time and then practiced in groups of three at a time. (3 items per 30 to 45-minute learning period.) To begin, say each of the three new vocabulary items (in isolation) and convey meaning through translation, gestures, props, pictures and/or mini-scenarios. At times a simple illustration will suffice, but confusion and miscommunication can be avoided by giving a direct translation (if and when it is possible). The brain can recall visual images much more efficiently than an isolated vocabulary item that is not contextualized and/or presented in a visual manner, so always follow up a translation with a visual representation of the new vocabulary structure.

Once students understand the meaning of the new vocabulary structure, begin teaching the associated gesture. First, say the new word or phrase and then model the appropriate gesture for your students. Say the new structure again and observe your students as they do the gesture without you. When you are certain that students know the meaning of the vocabulary structure and the corresponding gesture, introduce the next two vocabulary items with the same process: teach the meaning of each structure and the corresponding gesture.

The introduction phase lends itself to practice via gestures. Using the new vocabulary structures, give students a variety of commands to which they will respond with the specified gesture. Keep in mind that the older the student, the less time will be spent on gestures. High school students will spend only two to five minutes practicing via gestures. The following commands will help you while you are in the introduction or gesture phase:

- **Novel commands** are commands/narrations that include new words or new combinations of words which students have not heard before. Any new or unknown item can be used for TPR practice as long as it is made comprehensible. If *'(s)he eats'* is one of the new vocabulary items, then typical commands might include: Eat a taco. Eat a big taco. Eat fast. Eat slow.
- **Play commands** are silly commands which should be used to practice vocabulary and/or to liven up a dragging class. Play commands might include: *Eat your big toe. Eat your nose. Eat your pencil. Eat your homework.*
- **Chain commands** include two to three new vocabulary items at one time. They enhance long-term retention by facilitating the use of mental imagery, as students find it necessary to visualize each portion of the command in order to successfully complete it. Using *'(s)he is hungry, (s)he eats, the wolf*, chain commands might include: *he is hungry, he eats; he is hungry, he eats, the wolf; the wolf, (he) eats, (he) is hungry; the wolf, is hungry, he eats.*

Assess students, and when they are ready, move on to *contextualized* practice via Personalized Questions and Answers (PQA) and Personalized Mini-Situations (PMS). Focusing on the new vocabulary items, ask students questions that pertain to their personal experiences, likes and dislikes, and individual personalities. For example, using the three new vocabulary items *(s)he is hungry, (s)he eats, the wolf,* the following questions will help students to personally relate to the new vocabulary: *Are you hungry? Do you eat liver? What do you like to eat? Do you eat wolf?* Once questioning becomes predictable, students will pay attention only when it is their turn to answer. Be sure to make questions interesting and humorous and use students' answers as a source of information for your PMS.

The purpose of the PMS is to provide more CI in a contextualized format. Since the average language learner needs to hear a word 50 to 75 times before it is internalized, the goal is to *cooperatively* create a PMS, and in so doing, provide as many repetitions as is necessary for acquisition to take place.

A PMS should contain no more than one to three new vocabulary items and three to four basic events/ideas. The following is an example of a PMS based on the following new vocabulary items: *(s)he is hungry, (s)he eats, the wolf. There is a wolf. The wolf is hungry. The wolf goes to the cafeteria and sees (student in the class). The wolf eats his/her pickle. Now (student) is hungry.*

Have students read the 'simplified' PMS after you have introduced it. The PMS must be told and retold a number of times to ensure that students internalize the vocabulary structures. Eventually, they should be able to verbalize ideas and facts about the story. Each time it is retold, small details should be ascertained from students through PQA and then added to the story. (Blaine Ray, the innovator of 'storytelling,' refers to this as "climbing the ladder of specificity.") The process becomes one of story-questioning, rather than story-telling.

There is a wolf. What is the wolf like? Is the wolf big or small? Yes, the wolf is big. There is a <u>big</u> *wolf. How does he feel? The wolf feels sad? NO, the wolf is not sad. (etc.) Is the wolf hungry? Yes, the wolf is hungry. The wolf is* <u>very hungry</u>. *The wolf goes to the cafeteria. What time does the wolf go to the cafeteria? The wolf goes* <u>at 9 A.M.,</u> *but there is no one there. Then the wolf goes* <u>at lunch time</u>. *Does the wolf see anyone? Yes. Who does the wolf see? Oh, the wolf sees (student in the class). Does the wolf see anyone else? He does? Who else does the wolf see? The wolf sees* <u>David</u>, *but David doesn't have any food. The wolf is very hungry, so he runs to* <u>Mary</u> *instead. Why does the wolf run to Mary? Because Mary is pretty?! No! Because she has a pickle? Is it a small pickle? No! Mary has a* <u>huge</u> *pickle. It's* <u>a foot long</u>! *The wolf eats her pickle. Does the wolf eat the WHOLE pickle? No, he eats* <u>most</u> *of the pickle, but leaves a small piece. How does Mary feel?* <u>She is angry, very angry.</u> *She is hungry too! She is* <u>so hungry she could eat a wolf!</u>

The story is continually embellished via PQA/student input until every possible detail is added. Once the story is complete, with every detail added, students will step away from their version of the PMS in order to READ the teacher's version (a PMS which is created as part of preparation for the lesson). The teacher's version of the PMS will not match the students' version. This is completely acceptable, because the focus is on teaching language, <u>not</u> on teaching a specific story. Each version should contain numerous repetitions of the new vocabulary structures.

In addition to PQA, PMS and reading, you may choose to incorporate other input-based activities into the lesson. (i.e.: cooperative activities and games, music and songs, chants, rhymes, etc.) The process of teaching three vocabulary structures is repeated until all new vocabulary items have been introduced/practiced (a min. of 50-75 repetitions). Once vocabulary is internalized, it is helpful to have learners engage in partner practice. Partner practice is a quick and easy way for students to practice identifying and verbalizing the new vocabulary. One partner says the word while the other gives the corresponding gesture. Or, one partner gives the gesture, and the other says the word. Observe and assess, and if students are ready, move on to the mini-story.

Step Two
Use the vocabulary in a story.
Like the PMS, mini-stories give new vocabulary meaning and context; they are a vehicle to recycle the vocabulary structures which were pre-taught via PMS. Mini-stories serve as a safety net of sorts, providing more meaningful and contextualized repetitions of the target vocabulary.
Introduce the story using visuals to accurately depict the storyline. Props, puppets, live actors, large illustrations and overhead transparencies will appeal to the right brain in addition to keeping your students' attention. If live actors are used to depict the story, make sure explicit instructions are given about the emotions to be displayed, dialogue within the script, exact locations of people and places in the story, specific movements, and so on.

Successful stories:

Contain *managed* vocabulary:
- 6 to 12 items per mini-story; 3 items per PMS.

Revolve around a hook or a conflict:
- **HOOKS:** current or local events; humor and/or exaggerated details; one silly or bizarre word; known characters, such as teachers, principals, and/or celebrities.
- **CONFLICT:** a problem to be solved; a mission to be accomplished.

Should be personalized:
- include responses from PQA and student input.
- based on students' interests.

Include a necessary and level-appropriate grammatical structure.

Begin by telling the story as simply as possible. Tell and retell the story several times, adding a few minor details each time you tell it. For example, add color, size and other adjectives, adverbs, location, names, etc. Students must hear the story numerous times until they are able to retell it and/or able to communicate naturally using the newly acquired language structures. Use the following techniques to perpetuate the story:

1. Shift from storytelling to story-questioning: Ask yes/no and either/or questions; tell a portion of the story and wait for students to fill in the blanks with the appropriate word or phrase; ask short-answer questions; make mistakes and wait for students to verbally make corrections.
2. Read the story: Partners, groups or class reads the story; complete written extension activities; create extension activities.
3. Co-op Retells: Point to an illustration and have students tell that part of the story; tell the story one segment at a time with no details and have students add as many details as possible.

As you retell the story, assess constantly. Susan Gross encourages constant assessment by "teaching to the eyes." Students' eyes will tell you if they understand, are interested, (dis)agree, etc. Another easy evaluation technique is to focus on a "Barometer Student," a term used by Blaine Ray. The "Barometer Student" refers to a student who is slightly below average, roughly in the fortieth percentile. The acquisition rate of a "Barometer Student" is often an ideal indicator of how to pace your class, as the rate is slow enough to keep the majority of your lower students engaged and fast enough to avoid boring the top half of the class.

Once students appear comfortable with the vocabulary/the story, initiate a partner practice. At this stage, the purpose of partner practice is to encourage students to practice telling the mini-story in a low-stress environment. Encourage student-partners to help each other, observe as they tell the story, and be available to model vocabulary structures. Assess constantly as you walk around the room and eavesdrop on their retells. Encourage students to self assess and ask for partner assessments as well. Simply ask students to rate each other or themselves on a scale of one to five. Follow the "Rule of 80-80." Eighty percent of your students should be able to retell the story with 80% accuracy. Once this is accomplished, an optional activity may be to have students write the story (in their own words).

Writing the mini-story helps students prove just how much they have accomplished and provides an outlet to use language creatively. However, it does little to enhance language acquisition, because it is an <u>output</u> activity. Nevertheless, writing is an important skill that can easily be developed through TPRS. The transition to writing is greatly simplified by doing a few of the following activities with your students first: read, read, READ! Read the PMS's together. Read the story together. Have students copy the story. Read the story sentences out of sequence and have students rewrite them in the correct order. Read and complete a variety of extension activities with the class. In addition to preparing students to write, these input activities will also enhance students' ability to retell the story and create revisions.

Step Three
Revise the mini-story and intensify acquisition.

Creating story revisions and intensifying acquisition is the last step to TPRS. Revising stories requires the language learner to "transfer" newly acquired language to other situations and/or creatively use it in a different context. A revision may consist of a prequel to a story (what happened before the story), a sequel (what happened after the story), an original story, a flashcard story (created from a mixture of newly acquired vocabulary and recycled vocabulary), a poem, a song, or an introduction to new grammar.

Beginning language learners typically need some direction and assistance when creating revisions, but after hearing a few teacher-generated revisions, students will soon create and retell on their own. Although beginners may not be able to tell a complete revision, they will provide creative ideas and details to create an entertaining revision.

Revisions provide a perfect solution for introducing new verb forms and tenses. For example, if the original vocabulary list included the verbs *he is hungry* and *he eats,* the revised vocabulary list for the revision could be converted to introduce first person singular or past tense: *I am hungry, I eat or he was hungry, he ate.* All grammar is treated as new vocabulary, and the entire TPRS process is repeated from the beginning. Only one verb form/tense is introduced at a time, and only mastered verbs are retaught in a new form or tense. Practice the new vocabulary (which in this case is a new form or tense), tell and retell the revision, and then further intensify acquisition with any of the following activities.

- Create an episode to an ongoing soap opera after each new group of vocabulary items is mastered.
- Present a related cultural lesson or a thematic unit.
- Incorporate technology with Internet research projects and PowerPoint® story presentations.
- And most importantly, read, read, READ!

When each of the three steps to the method is incorporated into the language classroom, TPRS aligns itself with the proven pedagogical principles supported by many respected experts, including Asher, Krashen, Gardner, and Hunter. It is also compatible with Bloom's Taxonomy.

- Knowledge: Knowing the literate translation of a word.
- Comprehension: Understanding meaning and how/when vocabulary is used.
- Application: Being able to use vocabulary appropriately in a story.
- Analysis: The ability to determine appropriate social setting and context.
- Synthesis: Creative use of vocabulary; circumlocution.
- Evaluation: Revising, editing, paraphrasing, rewording.

Each step follows a logical and pedagogically sound sequence. By following each one, you will ensure that essential conditions are met for successful, rapid, and lasting language acquisition.

Wer bist du?
ERSTE STUFE

Wortschatz

neu
in der Schule
jetzt
in der Deutschklasse

die Deutschlehrerin
heißt, heißen
Frau

das, die Mädchen
die Jungen
Prima!

Minigeschichte

Rudi ist neu in der Schule. Er ist jetzt in der Deutschklasse. Die
Deutschlehrerin heißt Frau Teuber. Wie heißen die Mädchen und die Jungen?
Und wie heißt das Mädchen da? Anja? Prima!

Wer bist du?
ZWEITE STUFE

Wortschatz

fragt	hier	Jahre
sagt	alt	froh

Minigeschichte

Rudi fragt das Mädchen: „Wie heißt du?" Das Mädchen sagt: „Ich heiße Anja. Und du?" „Ich heiße Rudi. Ich bin neu hier in der Schule." Anja sagt: „Ich bin auch neu. Wie alt bist du?" Rudi sagt: „Ich bin 15 Jahre alt. Wie alt bist du?" Anja sagt: „Ich bin auch 15!" Rudi ist froh.

Wer bist du?
DRITTE STUFE

Wortschatz

kommt	mit dem Rad	mit dem Moped
Hauptstadt	mit dem Bus	zusammen
zu Fuß		

Minigeschichte

Woher kommt Anja? Sie kommt aus München, der Hauptstadt von Bayern. Rudi kommt auch aus Bayern, aus Augsburg. Anja kommt zu Fuß, mit dem Rad oder mit dem Bus zur Schule. Rudi ist jetzt 16 Jahre alt und kommt mit dem Moped. Rudi und Anja kommen zusammen mit dem Moped zur Schule. Prima!

ERSTE STUFE

TPR Gestures

neu mime rocking a baby
in der Schule place arms in peak above head and then point at a book
jetzt point emphatically at watch
in der Deutschklasse touch wall of classroom
die Deutschlehrerin point to self *or* point to self and then run thumb down jawline
heißt, heißen run finger along front of shirt just below collarbone, as though pointing to a name tag
Frau run thumb down jawline and then hold hand horizontally above head
das, die Mädchen run thumb down jawline and then hold hand horizontally below shoulder
die Jungen run fingers from forehead outward, as if along the bill of a baseball cap, and then hold hand horizontally below shoulder
Prima! hold both thumbs up and smile

Teaching Suggestion

- Have a student play the role of Rudi and introduce himself to students in the class. Students should respond with German names.

Additional Vocabulary

Herr run fingers from forehead outward, as if along the bill of a baseball cap
der Deutschlehrer point to self *or* point to self and then run fingers from forehead outward, as if along the bill of a baseball cap

ZWEITE STUFE

TPR Gestures

fragt touch mouth with fingers, draw hand away from face, and draw a question mark in the air
sagt touch mouth with fingers and draw hand away from face
hier point toward feet
alt mime walking with a cane
Jahre circle right fist around left fist, indicating earth's revolution
froh frame smiling face with open hands

Teaching Suggestion

- Have a student play the role of Anja and ask other students for their ages.

DRITTE STUFE

TPR Gestures

kommt move two fingers in walking motion toward self
Hauptstadt trace outline of a city skyline with finger and point to head
zu Fuß take a few short steps while pointing toward feet
mit dem Rad lean forward with arms out as though holding handlebars
mit dem Bus mime driving a bus (large steering wheel)
mit dem Moped hold arms out straight as though holding handlebars and weave upper body back and forth
zusammen hook index fingers together

Teaching Suggestions

- You may substitute any of the vocabulary on page 30 for the modes of transportation mentioned in the **Minigeschichte.**

- Cardboard replicas of German signs can be used to replace certain gestures, i.e., the sign for a bus stop can be used to illustrate **mit dem Bus.** When you say **mit dem Bus,** students should point to the sign.

Additional Vocabulary

mit dem Auto mime driving a car
mit der U-Bahn draw a U in the air and then extend hand, palm down, to convey motion

Spiel und Spaß
ERSTE STUFE

Wortschatz

macht … Sport	Fußball	spielt Klavier
Freizeit	hat	Schach
spielt … Tennis	Interessen	Gitarre

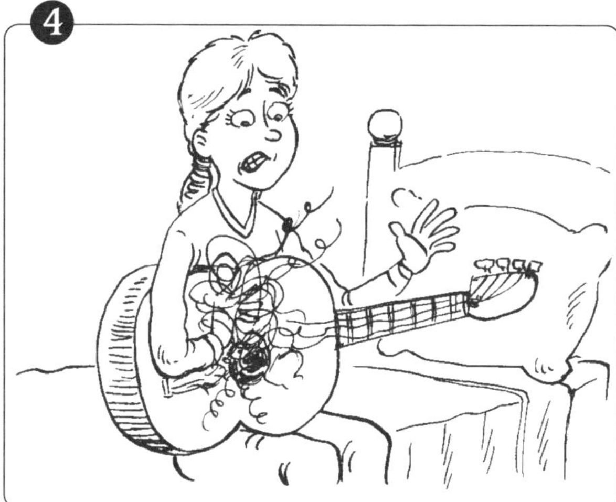

Minigeschichte

Gisela macht viel Sport in ihrer Freizeit. Sie spielt oft Tennis und Fußball.
Sie hat auch andere Interessen: sie spielt Klavier und Schach. Gitarre spielt
sie nicht.

Spiel und Spaß
ZWEITE STUFE

Wortschatz

besucht ... Freunde	schaut ... Fernsehen	wandert
nicht gern	tanzt	sammelt ... Briefmarken
hört ... Musik	schwimmt	sehr gern

Minigeschichte

Dieter besucht nicht gern Freunde. Er hört nicht gern Musik, schaut nicht gern Fernsehen und tanzt nicht gern. Dieter schwimmt und wandert auch nicht so gern. Er sammelt aber sehr gern Briefmarken.

Spiel und Spaß
DRITTE STUFE

Wortschatz

findet Golf toll
am Wochenende
Comics
findet ... Spitze

sammelt
am Nachmittag
zeichnen, zeichnet
macht ... Spaß

am Abend
macht ... die Hausaufgaben
langweilig

Minigeschichte

Lu findet Golf toll. Das spielt sie oft am Wochenende. Comics findet sie Spitze, und sie sammelt Comics am Nachmittag. Zeichnen macht auch Spaß. Sie zeichnet gern am Abend. Am Abend macht Lu auch die Hausaufgaben. Das findet sie aber langweilig.

ERSTE STUFE

TPR Gestures
macht Sport jump up and down one time
Freizeit cover watch with hand
spielt Tennis mime playing tennis
Fußball mime playing soccer
hat make a fist
Interessen hold fingers to temples
spielt Klavier mime playing the piano
Schach mime playing chess
Gitarre mime strumming a guitar

Teaching Suggestions
- You may substitute any of the vocabulary on page 45 for the activities in the **Minigeschichte.**
- Ask students to personalize the story and perform their version for the class.

Additional Vocabulary
spielt Basketball mime tossing a basketball at the hoop
spielt Golf mime playing golf
spielt Karten mime dealing out cards

ZWEITE STUFE

TPR Gestures
besucht Freunde mime opening a door; look surprised and happy
nicht gern frown and shake head
hört Musik cup hand around ear
schaut Fernsehen mime using a remote control
tanzt mime dancing
schwimmt mime swimming
wandert mime hooking thumb through backpack strap and walk a few steps
sammelt Briefmarken mime licking stamp and pasting it in book
sehr gern smile and nod emphatically

Teaching Suggestions
- Have students substitute other vocabulary from page 49 in the **Minigeschichte** in order to personalize the tale. They should make up their own gestures for the vocabulary in the **Und dann noch ...** box. Ask them to tell their version to the class.
- Ask true/false questions about the story, substituting other vocabulary from this **Stufe.** Have students correct false statements.

Additional Vocabulary
bastelt mime painting a model
schreibt mime writing
geht schwimmen mime throwing a towel over shoulder

DRITTE STUFE

TPR Gestures
findet Golf toll mime swinging a golf club while smiling happily
am Wochenende point to watch and then wipe back of hand across brow as though relieved
Comics hold up thumb and index finger close together (to indicate thinness of comic books) and then mime flipping pages
findet Spitze point to something, then give thumbs up sign
sammelt draw arms toward self, as though gathering something in
am Nachmittag point to watch and hold up three fingers
zeichnen, zeichnet mime sketching
macht Spaß bend arms at elbow and flap them up and down
am Abend point to watch and then hold up seven fingers
macht die Hausaufgaben mime opening book and writing
langweilig open mouth and pat hand against it, as though yawning

Teaching Suggestions
- You might want to use a cardboard clock face with adjustable hands instead of gestures to indicate time expressions.
- Substitute seasons for the time expressions

Additional Vocabulary
nach der Schule mime looking at watch and closing book
im Frühling mime opening window
im Sommer mime fanning self
im Herbst mime raking leaves
im Winter mime shoveling snow
interessant rest chin on fist
blöd thumbs down
macht keinen Spaß shake head while bending arms at elbow and flapping them up and down

Komm mit nach Hause!
ERSTE STUFE

geht	auf dem Land	essen, isst
nach Hause	möchte	trinken, trinkt
weit von hier	ein Stück Kuchen	Obst
wohnt		

Minigeschichte

Andrea geht nach der Schule zu Fuß nach Hause. Das ist weit von hier. Sie wohnt auf dem Land. Jetzt möchte sie ein Stück Kuchen essen und eine Cola trinken. Sie isst aber Obst und trinkt ein Mineralwasser. Das macht keinen Spaß!

Komm mit nach Hause!
ZWEITE STUFE

Wortschatz

seine Möbel
der Stuhl
sitzen

unbequem
der Schreibtisch
klein

die Stereoanlage
kaputt

Minigeschichte

Ahmet hat seine Möbel nicht gern. Er möchte auf dem Stuhl sitzen, aber der
Stuhl ist alt und unbequem. Er möchte basteln, aber der Schreibtisch ist klein.
Er möchte Musik hören, aber die Stereoanlage ist kaputt! Ahmet geht
schwimmen.

Komm mit nach Hause!
DRITTE STUFE

Wortschatz

lange, schwarze Haare
haben
seine Schwester

seine Mutter
kurze, blonde Haare
sein Vater

eine Glatze
sein Großvater
aussehen, sieht ... aus

Minigeschichte

Im Winter möchte Jens lange, schwarze Haare haben wie seine Schwester und
seine Mutter. Im Frühling möchte er kurze, blonde Haare haben wie sein
Vater. Im Sommer möchte Jens eine Glatze haben wie sein Großvater. Jetzt
sieht er aber interessant aus!

ERSTE STUFE

TPR Gestures

geht move two fingers in walking motion away from self

nach Hause form peak with hands, bring to cheek

weit von hier place hand horizontally above eyes and squint, as though looking at something far away

wohnt raise arms above head, hands touching to form a peak

auf dem Land mime hooking thumbs through suspenders while rocking back and forth

möchte extend hand palm up and close fingers

ein Stück Kuchen mime cutting a cake

essen, isst mime eating

trinken, trinkt mime drinking

Obst mime picking fruit from a tree

Teaching Suggestions

- A picture can be used to replace certain gestures; i.e., a picture of the countryside can be used to illustrate **auf dem Land**.

- You may substitute any of the vocabulary on pages 69 and 71 for the locations, foods, and drinks in the **Minigeschichte**.

Additional Vocabulary

in der Stadt trace outline of a city skyline with finger

Apfelsaft/Orangensaft mime picking fruit from tree, and then mime drinking

gar nichts wave hands in front of body as though rejecting something

ZWEITE STUFE

TPR Gestures

die Möbel gesture around room at all the furniture

der Stuhl point to a chair

sitzen sit down

unbequem move shoulders as though clothing is uncomfortable

der Schreibtisch point to teacher's desk

klein bend forward slightly and pull arms in toward chest to reduce physical size

die Stereoanlage make turning motion with hand, as though turning radio dial

kaputt make fists and turn them quickly downward, as though breaking a pencil

Teaching Suggestion

- Have students practice the gestures for the four pairs of antonyms in conjunction with each other.

Additional Vocabulary

groß spread arms wide to either side

bequem lean back and close eyes as though comfortable

schön hold hand up in front of face as though looking into mirror and smile

hässlich hold hand in front of face as though looking into a mirror and frown

DRITTE STUFE

TPR Gestures

lange, schwarze Haare mime running your fingers through long hair, then point to something black in the classroom

haben make a fist

seine Schwester run thumb down jawline and then hold bent arm out to side, as though walking arm in arm with someone

seine Mutter run thumb down jawline while holding other arm as though rocking a baby

kurze, blonde Haare mime running your fingers through short hair, then point to something yellow or beige in the classroom

sein Vater run fingers from forehead outward, as if along the bill of a baseball cap, while holding other arm as though rocking a baby

eine Glatze rub top of head

sein Großvater mime walking with a cane while holding other arm as though rocking a baby

aussehen, sieht ... aus gesture to self

Teaching Suggestion

- You may substitute any of the vocabulary on page 77 for the family members in the **Minigeschichte**.

Additional Vocabulary

der Hund hold hands up before body and pant

die Katze mime stroking whiskers

die Augen point to eyes

eine Brille make circles with thumb and index finger of each hand and hold before eyes

Alles für die Schule!
ERSTE STUFE

wieder
Geschichte
dieses Fach
dann

Bio
Kunst
danach
Mathe

eine Pause
sucht
(der) Stundenplan
zuletzt

Minigeschichte

Im Herbst geht Renate wieder zur Schule. Am Montag um acht Uhr hat sie Geschichte. Dieses Fach hat sie sehr gern. Dann hat sie Bio und Kunst. Kunst macht keinen Spaß. Danach hat sie Mathe. Sie findet die Mathelehrerin toll. Um elf Uhr dreißig hat sie eine Pause. Nach der Pause sucht sie den Stundenplan, aber sie findet ihn nicht! Welches Fach hat sie denn zuletzt?

Alles für die Schule!
ZWEITE STUFE

Wortschatz

bekommt
seine Noten
eine Eins

eine Zwei
eine Drei
eine Vier

eine Fünf
schlecht

Minigeschichte

Am Freitag bekommt Matthias seine Noten. Er geht nach der Schule nach
Hause und sagt: „Hallo, Mutti! Ich habe eine Eins in Latein und Bio. In
Geschichte habe ich eine Zwei und in Sport eine Drei." „Und was hast du in
Erdkunde und Deutsch?", fragt die Mutter. Matthias sagt: „In Deutsch bloß
eine Vier und in Erdkunde eine Fünf." „Das ist schlecht, mein Sohn", sagt die
Mutter. „Heute Abend besuchst du deine Freunde nicht. Du machst deine
Hausaufgaben."

4 Alles für die Schule!
DRITTE STUFE

Wortschatz

Schulsachen
die Hefte
die Kulis
billig
die Taschenrechner

preiswert
die Schultaschen
teuer
kosten

20 Euro
viel Geld
kauft
nimmt

Minigeschichte

Ingrids Schulsachen sind hässlich und alt, und sie möchte neue. Die Hefte
und die Kulis sind billig, und die Taschenrechner sind auch ganz preiswert.
Die Schultaschen sind aber ziemlich teuer; sie kosten 20 Euro. Ingrid hat aber
nicht viel Geld, nur 4 Euro. Sie kauft nichts. Ihr Bruder Holger hat schon neue
Schulsachen; sie geht nach Hause und nimmt sie.

ERSTE STUFE

TPR Gestures

wieder twirl index fingers around each other

Geschichte stand with hand held flat against lower chest, as in a Napoleonic pose

dieses Fach write names of school subjects on blackboard and point to it

dann hold up thumb and index finger, and touch index finger

Bio mime using a microscope

Kunst mime painting

danach hold up thumb, index, and middle finger; touch middle finger

Mathe draw a hyperbole in the air

eine Pause cross arms and take a deep breath

sucht mime searching through a pile of clothes

(der) Stundenplan hold up one hand and run finger down palm, as though reading through a list

zuletzt hold up little finger and touch with other hand

Teaching Suggestions

- Explain the meaning of **heute Abend** before you tell the story,

- You may substitute any of the vocabulary on page 97 for the school subjects in the **Minigeschichte.**

- You might want to use a cardboard clock face with adjustable hands instead of gestures to indicate time expressions.

- Ask students to personalize the story and perform their version for the class.

Additional Vocabulary

Deutsch gesture around classroom

Englisch hold up an English-language novel

Erdkunde mime spinning a globe

Latein encircle forehead with index fingers and thumbs, keeping the rest of the fingers spread out (should resemble a laurel wreath)

Sport mime bouncing a ball

ZWEITE STUFE

TPR Gestures

bekommt hold hands out in front of body and then bring them in to chest, as though receiving a gift

seine Noten hold up all fingers in sequence, starting with the thumb

eine Eins hold up one finger (thumb)

eine Zwei hold up two fingers

eine Drei hold up three fingers

eine Vier hold up four fingers

eine Fünf hold up five fingers

schlecht thumbs down

Teaching Suggestion

- Ask true/false questions about the story, substituting other vocabulary from this **Stufe.** Have students correct false statements.

Additional Vocabulary

Lieblings- hold hand over heart and then use gesture for specific subject

DRITTE STUFE

TPR Gestures

Schulsachen point to student's school supplies

die Hefte hold up notebook

die Kulis mime clicking a ball-point pen

billig rub thumb against fingers of same hand and then hold hand at waist level

die Taschenrechner mime using a calculator

preiswert rub thumb against fingers of same hand and then hold hand at chest level

die Schultaschen mime throwing a backpack over shoulder

teuer rub thumb against fingers of same hand and then hold hand above head

kosten rub thumb against fingers of same hand and then extend hand as though paying

20 Euro rub thumb against fingers of same hand and point to poster/map of Germany

viel Geld rub thumb against fingers of same hand as though counting money

kauft mime handing money to a cashier and receiving something

nimmt mime snatching something

Teaching Suggestion

- You may substitute any of the vocabulary on page 106 for the school supplies in the **Minigeschichte.**

- You might want to point out that many of the terms in this **Stufe** are compound words: **Schule + Tasche = Schultasche; Wörter + Buch = Wörterbuch,** etc.

Additional Vocabulary

der Bleistift mime sharpening a pencil

das Buch hold up a book

die Kassette draw small circles in air, as though rewinding a tape manually

der Radiergummi mime erasing

das Wörterbuch hold up a dictionary

Klamotten kaufen
ERSTE STUFE

Klamotten	die Stiefel	(ein) Gürtel
braucht	(ein) Pulli	eine Hose
ein Hemd	Turnschuhe	eine Jacke
eine Jeans		

Minigeschichte

Thomas kauft gern neue Klamotten. Er braucht ein Hemd, eine Jeans und schwarze Stiefel. Das Hemd findet er aber ziemlich unbequem, und die Stiefel sind hässlich. Jetzt sucht er einen Pulli und weiße Turnschuhe. Diese Klamotten findet er toll. Er möchte auch einen Gürtel, eine Hose und eine Jacke kaufen. Das alles kostet aber viel zu viel!

Klamotten kaufen
ZWEITE STUFE

Wortschatz

gefallen

das T-Shirt

furchtbar

dieser Rock

scheußlich

weit

diese Bluse

hübsch

fesch

die Shorts passen

sieht ... aus

Minigeschichte

Monika bekommt die alten Klamotten von ihrer Schwester Gisela. Die Klamotten gefallen Monika überhaupt nicht. „Diese Hose ist mir viel zu lang, und das T-Shirt finde ich furchtbar", sagt sie. „Und dieser Rock! Er ist scheußlich und zu kurz, und dieser Pulli ist mir zu weit. Aber diese Bluse, sie ist hübsch, und die Stiefel sind fesch. Und die Shorts passen mir prima. Ja, das sieht wirklich gut aus!"

Klamotten kaufen
DRITTE STUFE

Wortschatz

nicht viel Zeit
anzuziehen (anziehen)

dunkel
probiert ... an

seine Socken

Minigeschichte

Karin besucht ihren Freund Kemal am Abend. Er hat nicht viel Zeit, seine guten Klamotten anzuziehen, und sein Zimmer ist dunkel. Er nimmt ein Hemd aus dem Schrank und probiert es an. Es passt ihm gut. Dann sucht er eine Hose. Er findet eine Jeans und zieht sie an. Danach zieht er seine Socken und seine Turnschuhe an. Karin ist jetzt da!

ERSTE STUFE

TPR Gestures
Klamotten tug at your own clothing
braucht place palms together and hold hands vertically at chest level
das Hemd mime buttoning up a shirt
eine Jeans mime hooking thumbs through belt loops
die Stiefel mime pulling on boots and then stomp once on floor
der Pulli mime pulling a sweater over head and run hand down arm to indicate long sleeves
Turnschuhe mime tying a shoelace
der Gürtel mime cinching up a belt
die Hose run finger down front of leg, as though along a pleat
die Jacke mime straightening out the collar of a jacket

Teaching Suggestion
- You might want to point to pictures of clothing items rather than using the gestures above.

Additional Vocabulary
der Jogging-Anzug mime pulling shirt on over head and then jog in place
das Kleid gesture from shoulder down to ankle

ZWEITE STUFE

TPR Gestures
gefallen mime hugging someone
das T-Shirt mime pulling a T-shirt over head and run hand halfway down upper arm to indicate short sleeves
furchtbar thumbs down
dieser Rock hold hand down at side, put thumb and fingers together, and raise arm out from body, as though pulling a skirt out to the side
scheußlich thumbs down and frown
weit spread arms out to each side

diese Bluse mime buttoning a shirt
hübsch hold hand up in front of face as though looking into mirror and smile
fesch place hand behind head and smile as though posing for a picture
die Shorts passen place hand just above knee-level, to indicate length of shorts, and smile while smoothing down shorts
sieht ... aus gesture to self

Teaching Suggestion
- You may substitute any of the vocabulary on page 121 for the clothing items in the **Minigeschichte,** and any vocabulary on page 126 for the adjectives.

Additional Vocabulary
ein bisschen hold thumb and index finger together and then draw apart while making a short tossing motion (as though adding a pinch of salt to a recipe)
eng hold arms tightly to sides of body
lässig shrug one shoulder
schick place hand behind head and smile as though posing for a picture
stark flex the muscles of one arm

DRITTE STUFE

TPR Gestures
nicht viel Zeit point to wall clock and make alarmed face
anzuziehen (anziehen) mime pulling on a pair of pants
dunkel mime tapping around in the dark
probiert ... an mime pulling on pants and then pretend to regard self critically in mirror
seine Socken mime pulling on socks

Teaching Suggestion
- Ask true/false questions about the story, substituting other vocabulary from this **Stufe.** Have students correct false statements.

Pläne machen
ERSTE STUFE

Viertel vor sieben	schlecht	fährt
so lala	Viertel nach acht	um halb neun
halb drei	miserabel	wieder

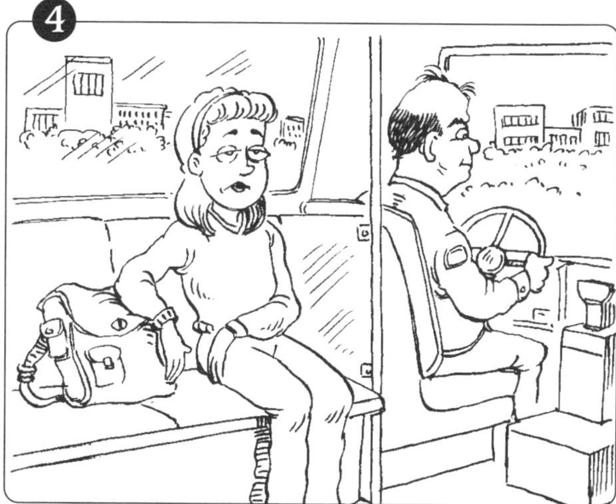

Minigeschichte

Am Samstagabend geht es Anke sehr gut. Sie ist froh, denn um Viertel vor sieben spielt sie Tennis mit ihren Freundinnen. Am Sonntagnachmittag geht es ihr so lala. Sie möchte um halb drei Klavier spielen, aber es ist kaputt. Es geht Anke am Sonntagabend schlecht. Sie macht ihre Hausaufgaben um Viertel nach acht, und das gefällt ihr überhaupt nicht. Am Montag geht es ihr miserabel, denn sie fährt um halb neun wieder in die Schule.

Pläne machen
ZWEITE STUFE

Wortschatz

wollen
in die Stadt gehen
fährt ... mit

ins Schwimmbad gehen
in ein Café gehen
Eis

ins Kino gehen
der Film
in eine Disko gehen

Minigeschichte

Nach der Schule wollen Svens Freunde in die Stadt gehen. Es geht Sven
ziemlich schlecht, aber er fährt trotzdem mit. Zuerst gehen sie ins
Schwimmbad. Dann gehen sie in ein Café und essen Eis. Danach gehen sie
ins Kino. Der Film ist furchtbar. Später gehen sie in eine Disko, aber Sven
geht es miserabel. Er fährt direkt nach Hause.

Pläne machen
DRITTE STUFE

nimmt … mit	schmeckt	Apfelkuchen
will	eine Nudelsuppe	(ein) Eisbecher
eine Pizza	ein Käsebrot	lecker

Minigeschichte

Jasmin nimmt ihren kleinen Bruder mit ins Café. Was will er essen? Eine
Pizza? Nein, Pizza schmeckt ihm nicht. Isst er vielleicht eine Nudelsuppe oder
ein Käsebrot? Das will er auch nicht. Möchte er denn ein Stück Apfelkuchen?
Nein! Will er einen Eisbecher? Jawohl! Eis findet er lecker.

ERSTE STUFE

TPR Gestures

Viertel vor sieben draw a quarter arc in the air, as though from three to twelve on a clock (from your point of view), and then hold up seven fingers

so lala hold hand in front of body and rotate quickly back and forth at the wrist

halb drei draw a half arc in the air and hold up three fingers

schlecht thumbs down

Viertel nach acht draw a quarter arc in the air, as though from twelve to nine on a clock (from your point of view), and then hold up eight fingers

miserabel thumbs down

fährt mime pushing on a gas pedal with right foot

um halb neun draw a half arc in the air and hold up nine fingers

wieder twirl index fingers around each other

Teaching Suggestions

- Have students rewrite and act out the story, using activities and times of their choosing.
- Ask true/false questions about the story, substituting other vocabulary from this **Stufe.** Have students correct false statements.

Additional Vocabulary

Wie spät ist es? / Wie viel Uhr ist es? point to watch and shrug

ZWEITE STUFE

TPR Gestures

wollen bring fist to chest

in die Stadt gehen move two fingers in walking motion away from self, and then trace outline of a city skyline

fährt ... mit hold steering wheel, mime pushing on a gas pedal, and then motion someone to join you

ins Schwimmbad gehen mime diving

in ein Café gehen mime opening a door while bringing other hand to mouth as though eating

Eis mime turning a handle, as on a home ice cream maker or mime licking an ice cream cone

ins Kino gehen mime opening a door and then mime filming with a video camera

der Film mime filming with a video camera

in eine Disko gehen mime opening! a door and then mime dancing

Teaching Suggestion

- Have students change the ending of the story and perform it for the class.

Additional Vocabulary

baden gehen mime swimming and then move two fingers in walking motion away from self

einen Film sehen mime filming and then mime putting on glasses

ins Konzert gehen mime playing a violin or directing an orchestra

DRITTE STUFE

TPR Gestures

nimmt ... mit mime snatching something and then mime walking away

will bring fist to chest

eine Pizza mime cutting a pizza

schmeckt lick lips and say "mmm"

eine Nudelsuppe mime stirring

ein Käsebrot form a triangle with hands and then mime cutting a loaf of bread

Apfelkuchen mime picking an apple and then pretend to take a bite of cake with a fork

(ein) Eisbecher mime dipping ice cream into a bowl

lecker rub stomach

Teaching Suggestion

- You may substitute any of the vocabulary on page 155 for the food vocabulary in the **Minigeschichte.**

Additional Vocabulary

ein Glas Tee mime sipping

eine Limo mime juicing a lemon by hand

eine Tasse Kaffee mime grinding up coffee beans

ein Wurstbrot mime grilling, and then mime cutting a loaf of bread

Zu Hause helfen
ERSTE STUFE

Wortschatz

muss	mäht den Rasen	gießt die Blumen
zu Hause	räumt ... auf	Staub saugen
helfen	putzt ... die Fenster	hat ... keine Zeit

Minigeschichte

Franz möchte zusammen mit seinen Freunden ins Kino gehen, aber zuerst muss er zu Hause helfen. Er mäht den Rasen und räumt schnell sein Zimmer auf. Danach putzt er die Fenster und gießt die Blumen. Am Abend muss er auch noch Staub saugen. Er hat einfach keine Zeit, einen Film zu sehen. Und er sieht jetzt ziemlich schlecht aus.

7 Zu Hause helfen
ZWEITE STUFE

Wortschatz

kann
tun
zweimal
deckt den Tisch

räumt ... ab
spült das Geschirr
manchmal
sortiert ... den Müll

füttert ... die Katze
heute
das Futter

Minigeschichte

Ulrike wohnt jetzt in der Nähe von ihren Großeltern. Was kann Ulrike für die Großeltern tun? Zweimal in der Woche kocht sie das Essen und deckt den Tisch für sie. Sie räumt den Tisch auch ab und spült das Geschirr. Manchmal sortiert sie den Müll, und jeden Tag füttert sie die Katze. Heute kann Ulrike das Futter für die Katze nicht finden! Was soll sie tun?

Zu Hause helfen
DRITTE STUFE

Wortschatz

Januar	warm	wolkig
das Wetter	trocken	Eis
die Sonne	kalt	auf den Straßen
scheint		

Minigeschichte

Es ist Januar, aber das Wetter ist trotzdem schön. Die Sonne scheint, und es ist warm und trocken. Jan besucht seine Freunde, und sie hören Musik und tanzen. Am Abend will Jan nach Hause fahren, aber das Wetter ist jetzt furchtbar. Es ist kalt und wolkig, und Eis ist auf den Straßen. Jan will deshalb nicht mit dem Bus fahren. Er geht zu Fuß nach Hause.

ERSTE STUFE

TPR Gestures

muss with a stern expression hold out hand and make a chopping motion

zu Hause form peak with hands, bring to cheek

helfen mime helping someone out of a chair

mäht den Rasen mime pulling the starter of a lawnmower and then pushing it

räumt ... auf mime picking up things from the floor and putting them in one spot

putzt ... die Fenster mime spraying and wiping the classroom window

gießt die Blumen mime watering plants

Staub saugen mime plugging in the vacuum cleaner and moving it in a back and forth motion

hat ... keine Zeit point to wristwatch and shake your head

Teaching Suggestions

- Have students substitute the chores for other chores they might have to do at home. Then have them retell the mini-story.

- Ask students to think about activities they would rather do. Then, in pairs, have them contrast the chore with the preferred activity using gestures.

Additional Vocabulary

das Bett machen mime straightening out a comforter and fluffing a pillow

ZWEITE STUFE

TPR Gestures

kann hold both hands in fists with the thumbs up in front of you so close that they touch

tun hold arms out and flap hands up and down fast

zweimal hold up index and middle finger briefly and then make an X with both index fingers

deckt den Tisch mime setting the table

räumt ... ab mime clearing the table

spült das Geschirr mime doing dishes

manchmal have arms in front and tap wristwatch with index finger twice

sortiert ... den Müll mime sorting trash into 3 containers

füttert ... die Katze kneel down handing food to an invisible cat saying "meow"

heute sweep hands palm down from center to either side; then, point index finger in a downward motion to the floor

kocht ... das Essen mime stirring

das Futter point to name of cat food written on the board

Teaching Suggestions

- Explain the meaning of **manchmal** before you tell the story.

- Ask students what else they do for their own grandparents and have them retell the story using their own gestures.

Additional Vocabulary

nie form an "X" with arms then undo in a sweeping motion with palm facing away from you

immer with index finger circle face of wristwatch several times

DRITTE STUFE

TPR Gestures

Januar point to "January" on calendar

das Wetter point to weather map

die Sonne motion a big circle with your hands above your head and look up

scheint shade eyes with hand looking up

warm mime taking off a jacket

trocken hold out palm as if to test for rain and shake head

kalt rub upper arms with opposite hands

wolkig point to clouds drawn on board

Eis with one foot mime testing ground for ice and nod

auf den Straßen point index finger to the floor, and then slide hands away from you with palms facing each other

Teaching Suggestions

- Ask students to come up with gestures for good-weather and bad-weather activities.

- Have students retell the **Minigeschichte** with the new vocabulary and gestures.

Additional Vocabulary

heiß mime wiping perspiration off your forehead

kühl mime pulling up the collar of a coat

nass mime shaking off water

sonnig smile upward shading your eyes

der Schnee mime picking up snow forming a snowball

der Regen mime opening an umbrella

der Grad point to thermometer (if not real then drawn on board)

8 Einkaufen gehen
ERSTE STUFE

einkaufen
soll
beim Bäcker
Semmeln

eine Torte
beim Metzger
Aufschnitt
holen

ein Hähnchen
im Supermarkt
(der) Kaffee
(die) Milch

Minigeschichte

Christa muss heute für ihre Mutter einkaufen gehen. Sie soll beim Bäcker
Semmeln kaufen, aber es gibt keine mehr. Sie kauft deshalb eine Torte. Beim
Metzger soll sie Aufschnitt holen, aber der sieht nicht gut aus. Sie kauft ein
Hähnchen. Im Supermarkt soll sie Kaffee kaufen, aber sie nimmt Milch. Ihre
Mutter findet das nicht gut.

Einkaufen gehen
ZWEITE STUFE

Wortschatz

Lebensmittel
bringen
(das) Kilo
Kartoffeln
(das) Pfund

Äpfel
im Obst- und Gemüseladen
zur Metzgerei
holt

(das) Hackfleisch
(die) Wurst
(der) Fisch
(der) Liter

Minigeschichte

Jürgen geht einmal in der Woche einkaufen. Er hat eine große Familie und muss deshalb viele Lebensmittel nach Hause bringen. Zuerst kauft er zwei Kilo Kartoffeln und vier Pfund Äpfel im Obst- und Gemüseladen. Dann geht er zur Metzgerei und holt ein Kilo Hackfleisch und ein halbes Kilo Wurst. Zuletzt kauft er drei Pfund Fisch und zwei Liter Milch. Wie soll er das alles mit dem Rad nach Hause fahren?

Einkaufen gehen
DRITTE STUFE

Wortschatz

weil	(die) Butter	(ein) Obstsalat
Trauben	(die) Eier	bleibt
Tomaten	(der) Zucker	
denn	(das) Mehl	

Minigeschichte

Heute Abend hat Gabi nichts zu tun. Ihre Freundin Anke kann nicht mit ihr ins Kino gehen, weil sie für ihre Großmutter Trauben und Tomaten kaufen muss. Gabis Freund Hans kann auch nicht mit ihr ins Kino gehen, denn er macht eine Torte und muss noch Butter, Eier, Zucker und Mehl kaufen. Gabis Bruder Jochen kann auch nicht mit, weil er einen Obstsalat für die Mutter macht. Gabi bleibt den ganzen Abend zu Hause und liest ein Buch von Hermann Hesse.

ERSTE STUFE

TPR Gestures

einkaufen mime giving someone money and taking something in return

soll move hands with palms facing each other in a short, abrupt downward motion in front of you

beim Bäcker with both hands, make outline of a store, then mime kneading bread dough

Semmeln mime cutting open a roll and spreading butter on it

eine Torte motion a circle with both hands on a table, then mime cutting out a piece

beim Metzger with both hands, make outline of a store, then mime chopping meat

Aufschnitt mime slicing ham in the palm of your hand

holen walk a few steps, mime picking something up, and then go back

ein Hähnchen flap bent arms as if they were wings

im Supermarkt mime walking down the aisle with a shopping cart and loading things into it

(der) Kaffee mime drinking from a mug

(die) Milch mime holding glass and say "moo"

Teaching Suggestion

- Have students create gestures for other food items found in Chapter 8.

Additional Vocabulary

das Brot form a sandwich with your hands, then point to the "bread" part of it

die Brezel outline a pretzel shape with your index fingers

ZWEITE STUFE

TPR Gestures

Lebensmittel mime eating then point to foods written on the board

bringen form a cup with both hands and mime taking it to someone while nodding

(das) Kilo motion "1" with index finger and mime holding something heavy

Kartoffeln mime peeling a potato; then motion elipses in the air for plural

(das) Pfund motion 1/2 with both index fingers and mime holding something heavy

Äpfel mime climbing up a ladder and picking an apple

im Obst- und Gemüseladen with both hands, make outline of a store, then mime peeling a banana

zur Metzgerei with both hands, make outline of a store, then mime chopping meat with a meat cleaver

holt point to a student, walk a few steps, pretend to pick something up, and then go back

(das) Hackfleisch point to the meat in a hamburger

(die) Wurst point to a picture of **Wurst**

(der) Fisch make a forward waving motion with your hand

(der) Liter indicate "1" with your fingers and mime pouring a liquid

Teaching Suggestion

- Explain the meaning of **Lebensmittel** before telling the story.

Additional Vocabulary

wiegen mime weighing something

ein bisschen indicate "a little" with thumb and index finger

DRITTE STUFE

TPR Gestures

weil twirl fist with extended index finger away from you

Trauben mime holding up a bunch of grapes and picking some off

Tomaten point to a picture of a tomato

denn same as **weil**

(die) Butter mime spreading butter on a slice of bread

Eier mime cracking open an egg then motion "1, 2, 3..." for plural

(der) Zucker mime spooning sugar in a mug then stirring it

(das) Mehl point to picture of flour

(ein) Obstsalat point to an apple and a pear drawn on the board then mime tossing

bleibt point to a student and hold up open hand with palm facing away from you

Teaching Suggestion

- Give students the meaning of **weil** and **denn** before starting the **Minigeschichte**.

Additional Vocabulary

heute Morgen gesture for **heute** and point to AM on board

heute Nachmittag gesture for **heute** and point to PM on board

Amerikaner in München
ERSTE STUFE

Wortschatz

im ... Hauptbahnhof
sieht
eine U-Bahnstation
die Innenstadt

das Rathaus
(der) Marktplatz
Kirchen
Museen

ein paar Stunden
eine Bank
geschlossen

Minigeschichte

Stephan ist jetzt im Münchner Hauptbahnhof. Er sieht eine U-Bahnstation und fährt in die Innenstadt. Dort findet er das Rathaus, den Marktplatz und viele schöne Kirchen. In der Nähe vom Marienplatz gibt es auch einige Museen. Nach ein paar Stunden sieht er eine Bank, und er will Geld holen. Die Bank ist aber geschlossen, weil es schon nach fünf Uhr ist. So ein Pech!

Amerikaner in München
ZWEITE STUFE

Wortschatz

der Englische Garten	nach rechts	danke
geradeaus	bis zum ... Platz	weiß
bis zur Ampel	direkt	weiter

Minigeschichte

Gisela ist in München und will den Englischen Garten besuchen. Sie fragt eine Frau, wo der Garten ist. Die Frau sagt: „Zuerst musst du geradeaus bis zur Ampel gehen. Dort geh nach rechts in die Ludwigstraße und dann wieder geradeaus bis zum Geschwister-Scholl Platz. Auf diesem Platz musst du nach rechts gehen. Der Englische Garten ist dann direkt vor dir." Gisela sagt danke, und sie geht geradeaus bis zur Ampel. Dann weiß sie nicht mehr weiter.

Amerikaner in München
DRITTE STUFE

Wortschatz

eine Imbissstube
Hunger
bayrisch(es)
probieren

eine Weißwurst
eine Vollkornsemmel
hungrig
(der) Leberkäs

mit Senf
überhaupt
ein Gyros
(das) Fleisch

Minigeschichte

John findet eine Imbissstube am Marienplatz. Er hat großen Hunger und möchte bayrisches Essen probieren. Zuerst isst er eine Weißwurst und eine Vollkornsemmel. Danach ist er immer noch hungrig und probiert Leberkäs mit Senf. Der Leberkäs schmeckt ihm überhaupt nicht. Zuletzt isst er noch ein Gyros. Jetzt ist er satt von dem vielen Fleisch.

ERSTE STUFE

TPR Gestures

im ... Hauptbahnhof make hissing sound of train then, motion "Stop" with open palm

sieht point index and middle fingers of right hand to eyes

eine U-Bahnstation point to **U-Bahnstation** sign on board

die Innenstadt make outline of a large circle horizontally to the floor; then point with index finger to the center of the circle

das Rathaus with both hands, make outline of a rectangle; then mime making a speech with raised finger

der Marktplatz make outline of a large circle horizontally to the floor; then use the gesture suggested for **einkaufen** in the **Erste Stufe** of Ch.8

Kirchen put both hands together to form the steeple of a church

die Museen outline rectangle for "building," then mime handling something with the utmost care (or write the name of a museum on the board and point to it)

ein paar Stunden point at clock and motion the hand going around three times

eine Bank outline a rectangle for "building" then rub fingers for "money"

geschlossen mime closing and locking a door

Teaching Suggestion

- Have students retell the **Minigeschichte** using the following vocabulary: **Hotel, Theater,** and **Post.**

Additional Vocabulary

die Post mime licking the flap of an envelope then putting a stamp on it

das Hotel outline a rectangle for "building," then mime sleeping

das Theater with both hands, make outline of a rectangle; then mime bowing in front of an audience

ZWEITE STUFE

TPR Gestures

der Englische Garten mime taking a leisurely stroll and smelling a flower

geradeaus point straight ahead

bis zur Ampel form three circles one after the other with index fingers and thumbs

nach rechts point right thumb to your right

bis zum ... Platz point away from you; then make outline of horizontal circle where you pointed

direkt put palms together and point away from you

danke lower your head and slowly bring it back up

weiß touch temple with index finger and move away swiftly

weiter swiftly move extended lower arm up and down twice

Teaching Suggestions

- Have students look at the map on p. 225 and give directions from the **Jugendclub** to the **Post** creating gestures where needed.

- Have students role-play the **Minigeschichte** in pairs.

Additional Vocabulary

nach links point left thumb to your left

DRITTE STUFE

TPR Gestures

eine Imbissstube outline small rectangle, then mime eating

Hunger rub your stomach with both hands

bayrisch(es) point to Bavaria on map

probieren mime testing the waters with your toe

eine Weißwurst point to "Weißwurst" written on the board

eine Vollkornsemmel form fist with one hand and dot it with other index finger several times (the grain)

hungrig rub your stomach with one hand

(der) Leberkäs show picture of **Leberkäs**

mit Senf mime squeezing mustard on a slice of bread (circular motion)

überhaupt nicht motion "no" with both index fingers

ein Gyros mime carving meat off a vertically rotating larger piece of meat

das Fleisch pinch your arm

Teaching Suggestion

- Explain what **Leberkäs** is before telling the story.

- Have students role-play a waitperson telling the chef two or three different orders. Have them create gestures as needed.

Additional Vocabulary

genug mime putting a hand over a glass

kein draw a '0' (zero) in the air

satt pat stomach with both hands

 10 Kino und Konzerte
ERSTE STUFE

Wortschatz

sehen	(der) Western	Sciencefictionfilme
mag	kennen	gar nicht
Krimis	die Schauspieler	die Oper

Minigeschichte

Sara, Rosi und Eva wollen ins Kino gehen und einen Film sehen. Sara mag Krimis, aber Rosi und Eva finden Krimis nicht gut. Rosi möchte den neuen Western sehen, aber Sara und Eva kennen die Schauspieler in diesem Film und finden sie furchtbar. Eva mag Sciencefictionfilme, aber solche Filme gefallen Sara und Rosi gar nicht. Die drei Mädchen gehen deshalb in die Oper *Die Zauberflöte.* Alle drei finden diese Oper gut.

 Kino und Konzerte
ZWEITE STUFE

die Komödie	(ein) Horrorfilm	am liebsten
lustig	meint	Actionfilme
phantasievoll	brutal	Abenteuerfilme
(ein) Kriegsfilm	grausam	spannend

Minigeschichte

Michael will heute Abend die Komödie *Airplane* sehen, weil er sie lustig und
phantasievoll findet. Sein Vater findet Komödien aber doof und möchte einen
Kriegsfilm oder Horrorfilm sehen. Michaels Mutter meint, dass Kriegsfilme
und Horrorfilme zu brutal und grausam sind. Sie mag am liebsten Actionfilme
und Abenteuerfilme, denn sie findet solche Filme spannend. Die ganze
Familie sieht dann einen alten Abenteuerfilm mit Harrison Ford.

10 Kino und Konzerte
DRITTE STUFE

Wortschatz

hat ... gelesen	(ein) Roman	(ein) Liebesroman
ein Sachbuch	(ein) Gruselroman	laut
(die) Politik	traurig	die Zeitung
(die) Umwelt		

Minigeschichte

Sophie hat am Wochenende ein Sachbuch über Politik und Umwelt gelesen.
Ihr Bruder Dieter hat einen Roman von Stephen King gelesen, einen
Gruselroman. Sophies Schwester hat einen traurigen Liebesroman gelesen.
Am Montagabend sprechen die Geschwister über die Bücher. Das gefällt dem
Vater nicht, weil die Geschwister ziemlich laut sprechen und der Vater die
Zeitung lesen will.

ERSTE STUFE

TPR Gestures
sehen point index and middle fingers to eyes
mag cup one hand with the other and pull to heart
Krimis hold one hand over eyes like a visor and other hand like holding a magnifying glass, make filming gesture: mime rolling the film on an old TV camera
(der) Western mime riding a horse and lassoing cattle, then make filming gesture
kennen while nodding several times, point to yourself, and then to another person
die Schauspieler mime bowing in front of an audience
Sciencefictionfilme trace two antennas on your head, then make filming gesture
gar nicht shake finger emphatically and shake head
die Oper mime singing loudly

Teaching Suggestions
• Have two students tell each other with types of movies they like and dislike and create gestures as needed.
• Have students retell a personalized version of the **Minigeschichte**.

Additional Vocabulary
der Liebesfilm bring palms to heart, then make filming gesture

ZWEITE STUFE

TPR Gestures
die Komödie put index fingers to corners of mouth and smile, then make filming gesture
lustig mime laughing out loud
phantasievoll mime saying "Ahh" and make a circular motion above head
ein Kriegsfilm march in place like a soldier, then make filming gesture
ein Horrorfilm peak out from behind hands, then make filming gesture
meint point index finger to temple
brutal make one punching motion
grausam mime twisting a rope with a vicious smile
am liebsten give thumb-up with one hand and point index finger of other hand to top of thumb
Actionfilme give a few short punches with

both arms, then make filming gesture
Abenteuerfilme mime being on the lookout with one hand shading eyes, then make filming gesture
spannend mime biting fingernails

Teaching Suggestion
• Explain **grausam** and **spannend** before telling the **Minigeschichte**.
• Ask students what the movie preferences of the members of their family are and have them retell a personalized version of the **Minigeschichte**.

Additional Vocabulary
lieber make thumb-up sign with one hand and move upward
sensationell make thumbs-up sign with both hands and move up and down twice
dumm/doof point index fingers to forehead and shake head

DRITTE STUFE

TPR Gestures
hat ... gelesen mime reading, then point right thumb backward over right shoulder
ein Sachbuch make book gesture: put opened palms together at the pinkies and mime reading; then, point to a "Bell curve" drawn on the board
(die) Politik mime giving a speech with raised index finger
(die) Umwelt with each hand draw a horizontal semicircle on each side of your body
(ein) Roman make book gesture, then flap palms together twice
(ein) Gruselroman make **Roman** gesture, then mime hiding behind your arm
(ein) Liebesroman make **Roman** gesture, then bring palms to heart
traurig mime wiping tears from your eyes
laut form a funnel in front of your mouth and mime yelling
die Zeitung mime holding a newspaper

Teaching Suggestion
• Have students rate a recent movie they saw using the adjectives given in the **Zweite Stufe**.

Additional Vocabulary
die Zeitschrift mime wetting your finger and then turning a page
das Hobbybuch make book gesture, then mime juggling

11 Der Geburtstag
ERSTE STUFE

Wortschatz

die Telefonzelle	steckt … ein	(ein) Moment
anrufen	die Münzen	wartet
hebt … ab	wählt	der Apparat
(der) Hörer	die Telefonnummer	

Minigeschichte

Klaus geht in die Telefonzelle, denn er möchte seinen Freund in Hannover anrufen. Er hebt den Hörer ab und steckt die Münzen ein. Dann wählt er die Telefonnummer. Ein Mann sagt: „Müller", und Klaus fragt: „Kann ich bitte Peter sprechen?" „Einen Moment, bitte", sagt der Mann. Klaus wartet. Jetzt braucht der Apparat mehr Geld, aber Klaus hat keine Münzen mehr! Was soll er tun?

Der Geburtstag
ZWEITE STUFE

feiert
zum ersten Mal
Chanukka

(der) Muttertag
(der) Vatertag
am zehnten Mai

(der) Geburtstag
eine Fete

Minigeschichte

Melina ist Amerikanerin, und sie wohnt dieses Jahr bei einer Familie in
Deutschland. Dort feiert sie zum ersten Mal Chanukka. Das findet sie sehr
interessant. Zum Muttertag kauft sie schöne Blumen für die Mutter, und zum
Vatertag kauft sie ein rotes Hemd für den Vater. Melina hat am zehnten Mai
Geburtstag, und ihre Familie macht eine Fete für sie. Melinas Freunde sollen
auch kommen. Das findet Melina Spitze!

Der Geburtstag
DRITTE STUFE

Wortschatz

Geschenkideen	(das) Parfüm	CDs
eine Armbanduhr	(der) Schmuck	falsch
Weihnachten	ein Poster	Geschenke
schenken		

Minigeschichte

Tobias hat viele Geschenkideen. Er will seinem Vater eine Armbanduhr zu Weihnachten schenken, und seiner Mutter will er Parfüm geben. Für seine Großmutter kauft er Schmuck, und für seinen kleinen Bruder kauft er ein Poster und CDs. Irgendwie bekommen sie aber die falschen Geschenke! Seiner Mutter schenkt Tobias das Poster und die CDs, und seinem Vater gibt er Parfüm. Seine Großmutter bekommt die Armbanduhr, und sein Bruder bekommt den Schmuck. So ein Mist!

ERSTE STUFE

TPR Gestures

die Telefonzelle outline an upright rectangle, then mime speaking on the phone

anrufen mime dialing, then speaking on the phone

hebt ... ab mime picking up the receiver of a phone

(der) Hörer form receiver with one hand, then point to it with other hand

steckt ... ein mime putting coins in a public phone

die Münzen mime pulling change out of your pocket and counting it

wählt mime punching a phone number on a key pad

die Telefonnummer point to phone number written on the board

(ein) Moment snap fingers to indicate an instant

wartet step in place with impatient expression on your face

der Apparat outline a small square against a wall and punch numbers on it

Teaching Suggestions

- Remind students that in Germany public phones are usually in booths. You might also want to mention that now most public phones require phone cards instead of coins.

- Have students retell the story with first having to call information for the number of a friend. They should create any additionally required gestures.

Additional Vocabulary

telefonieren same gesture as **anrufen**

das Telefon same gesture as **Apparat**

auflegen mime putting the receiver back on the phone

besetzt mime putting the receiver to your ear, then looking at it in disappointment, and hanging it back up (or imitate the busy signal tone)

ZWEITE STUFE

TPR Gestures

feiert dance with arms up and a happy face

zum ersten Mal signal '1' with index finger, then make 'x' with both index fingers

Chanukka point to picture of a Menorah

(der) Muttertag point to Mother's Day on calendar

(der) Vatertag point to Father's Day on calendar

(der) Geburtstag point to yourself then to your birthday on calendar

am zehnten Mai signal '10' with fingers and point to May on calendar

eine Fete mime hanging balloons, turning on music, and dancing

Teaching Suggestions

- Ask students what they usually do for Mother's Day and Father's Day and have them create gestures for it.

- Have students retell the personalized version of the **Minigeschichte** with their new gestures.

Additional Vocabulary

Ostern mime handpainting of an egg

DRITTE STUFE

TPR Gestures

Geschenkideen touch temple with index finger moving finger away swiftly, then mime tying a bow around a present

eine Armbanduhr point to the wrist band of a watch, but not to the face

Weihnachten point to Christmas tree drawn on the board

schenken mime giving a boxed gift to someone

(das) Parfüm mime spraying perfume behind your ears

(der) Schmuck point to ring, bracelet, or necklace

ein Poster point to poster on the classroom wall

CDs form a disc with both hand, then mime inserting it into a CD player

falsch form 'X' with arms, starting at elbow

Geschenke outline a box with a bow on top

Teaching Suggestions

- Ask students to think of gifts they like to give and have them create gestures for those gifts.

- Have students retell the story using different gift ideas.

Additional Vocabulary

die Praline mime picking one of a variety of candies from a box

der Kalender point to calendar

der Blumenstrauß mime smelling flowers

Die Fete
ERSTE STUFE

backen
nicht genau
benutzt
(der) Zimt

(das) Butterschmalz
(das) Öl
(das) Salz

Zwiebeln
Zitronen
wahrscheinlich

Minigeschichte

Sandra möchte einen Apfelkuchen für eine Fete backen, aber sie weiß nicht genau, wie man das macht. Sie benutzt beim Backen Zimt, Butterschmalz, Öl und ein bisschen Salz. Dann sucht sie Äpfel. Es sind aber keine im Haus! Sie hat keine Zeit, Äpfel zu kaufen, und deshalb benutzt sie Zwiebeln und Zitronen. Bei der Fete essen Sandras Freunde nicht viel Kuchen. Sandra meint, dass sie wahrscheinlich keinen Hunger haben.

Die Fete
ZWEITE STUFE

Wortschatz

aus ... Seide
geht in den Zoo
gepunktet
aus Leder

geht in den Park
joggen
gestreift

aus Baumwolle
läuft Schlittschuh
die Stadt besichtigen

Minigeschichte

Iwan weiß nie, welche Klamotten er anziehen soll. Er zieht ein teures Hemd aus blauer Seide an und geht in den Zoo. Er zieht eine gepunktete Hose aus Leder an und geht in den Park, um zu joggen. Manchmal zieht Iwan gestreifte Shorts aus Baumwolle an und läuft Schlittschuh. Heute will er die Stadt besichtigen. Wie sieht er jetzt aus?

Die Fete
DRITTE STUFE

Wortschatz

das Wohnzimmer	eckig	rund
Teppiche	(ein) Tisch	(ein) Esstisch
(ein) Sessel	aus Holz	aus Kunststoff
modern	eine Lampe	(ein) Kühlschrank
(ein) Sofa	die Küche	

Minigeschichte

Silvana hat jetzt eine Wohnung und möchte neue Möbel kaufen. Für das Wohnzimmer braucht sie zwei Teppiche, einen Sessel, ein modernes grünes Sofa und einen kleinen eckigen Tisch aus Holz. Sie möchte auch eine Lampe fürs Wohnzimmer haben. Für die Küche braucht sie einen runden Esstisch aus Kunststoff und einen großen Kühlschrank. Jetzt sind die Möbel hier, und sie muss für alles Platz finden!

ERSTE STUFE

TPR Gestures
backen mime kneading dough
nicht genau shake hand in 'not sure' type gesture
benutzt fold hands with fingers of one hand wrapped around other hand
(der) Zimt point to picture of cinnamon stick or powder
(das) Butterschmalz point to package of shortening
(das) Öl point to popular brand of oil written on the board
(das) Salz mime shaking salt on a dish
Zwiebeln mime cutting onions while wiping tears from your eyes
Zitronen mime biting into a lemon, and then make a 'sour' face
wahrscheinlich shake fist while making 'thumbs-up' sign

Teaching Suggestions
- Explain the meaning of **Butterschmalz** and **wahrscheinlich** before telling the **Minigeschichte**.
- Have students create gestures for additional ingredients needed for the **Apfelküchle** recipe on p. 298. Have them tell you the recipe using all necessary gestures.

ZWEITE STUFE

TPR Gestures
aus Seide touch the fabric of your sleeve, then point to 'silk' written on the board
geht in den Zoo kneel down and mime petting animals
gepunktet with index finger draw dots on your shirt or blouse
aus Leder touch the fabric of your jacket, then point to 'leather' written on the board
geht in den Park walk and point to 'park' written on the board
joggen mime jogging
gestreift with index finger draw stripes on your shirt or blouse
aus Baumwolle touch the fabric of your sleeve, then point to 'cotton' written on the board
läuft Schlittschuh mime skating
die Stadt besichtigen mime looking at a travel guide, then look up in recognition

Teaching Suggestions
- Explain **die Stadt besichtigen** before telling the **Minigeschichte**.
- Have students continue the mini-story by answering the question at the end. Then, have them retell the **Minigeschichte** with their own version for the ending.

Additional Vocabulary
ein Brettspiel spielen mime playing checkers

DRITTE STUFE

TPR Gestures
das Wohnzimmer point to a picture of a living room
Teppiche mime lifting the corner of a rug shaking it slightly
(ein) Sessel mime sitting in an armchair with arms crossed behind head
(ein) Sofa mime sitting down, then point to 'sofa' written on board
eckig outline a sharp corner with your hand
(ein) Tisch outline a table with your hands
aus Holz knock on wood
eine Lampe point to a lamp
die Küche mime tying an apron around your waist and rolling up sleeves
rund outline a rounded corner with your hand
(ein) Esstisch outline a table, then mime eating at it
aus Kunststoff point to something made of plastic
(ein) Kühlschrank mime opening the refrigerator, then shiver as if cold

Teaching Suggestions
- Draw a simple blueprint of a house with bedroom, den, kitchen, and bathroom on the board before telling the **Minigeschichte**. Give the meaning of **Wohnung**.
- Have students furnish each room of their new appartment, then have them retell the **Minigeschichte**.

Additional Vocabulary
der Herd mime holding hands over a stove
der Ofen mime opening the oven and act as if hot
das Spülbecken mime washing the dishes